T0148246

Chuckles:
Mild to Severe

Donald Lee Armentrout

iUniverse, Inc.
Bloomington

Chuckles: Mild to Severe

Copyright © 2011 by Donald Lee Armentrout

All rights reserved. No part of this book may be used or reproduced by any means, graphic, electronic, or mechanical, including photocopying, recording, taping or by any information storage retrieval system without the written permission of the publisher except in the case of brief quotations embodied in critical articles and reviews.

The views expressed in this work are solely those of the author and do not necessarily reflect the views of the publisher, and the publisher hereby disclaims any responsibility for them.

iUniverse books may be ordered through booksellers or by contacting:

iUniverse
1663 Liberty Drive
Bloomington, IN 47403
www.iuniverse.com
1-800-Authors (1-800-288-4677)

Because of the dynamic nature of the Internet, any web addresses or links contained in this book may have changed since publication and may no longer be valid.

Any people depicted in stock imagery provided by Thinkstock are models, and such images are being used for illustrative purposes only.

Certain stock imagery © Thinkstock.

ISBN: 978-1-4620-1782-9 (sc)
ISBN: 978-1-4620-1783-6 (e)

Library of Congress Control Number: 2011907509

Printed in the United States of America

iUniverse rev. date: 6/9/2011

Acknowledgments

I extend a sincere appreciation to everyone who, through the years, served as a source of material for this book. Special thanks are extended to Joan C. Frank for proofreading this project, and to Carol Weaver, who designed the cover.

Introduction

As a school principal, scoutmaster, and family man, my chuckles radar was constantly scanning. It is amazing how daily living provides an inexhaustible source of material resulting in smiles, chuckles, snorts, and laughs.

So what is this thing called a chuckle? Experts say it is a quiet inward laugh. I agree but believe an important sensation accompanies chuckles: momentary joy. I feel so good inside when I am able to chuckle. It is a thrill when I can share a story or comment on something seen or heard that causes someone to chuckle or laugh. There is definitely a chuckle process. It starts with a slight smile, and then a chuckle escapes, which leads to eyes twinkling and sometimes laughter.

Chuckles: Mild to Severe represents my journey of chuckles through the years. Most of the stories are true, but I did create some from my imagination. I have used an easy-to-read format that consists of short, concise stories and observations. Most are a couple paragraphs in length and others are a sentence or two.

I have organized the book into six parts. Part 1 contains my observations as a principal, watching students interact with teachers, each other, and me. There are, however, some stories given to me by fellow teachers, including my wife. Student behavior and comments reflect the mischievousness, creativity, and innocence (usually) of youth at different ages. In this part you will chuckle:

- While witnessing your house being wrapped in toilet paper

- When a middle school student needs a cup—and not for drinking.

- When observing a boy flossing with a sock—at his desk

- When learning that the proof is in the pudding

The emphasis of Part 2 is family stories that make people laugh. I've included personal vignettes, including events of my parents, my wife's parents, cousins, and others. In many cases, I used actual family names; however, some names are fictional in order that I might retain their friendship. Some of the items you will learn about in Part 2 include:

- How a child tests the quality of an apple

- The stork market

- Pizza in heaven

- Bearing all in Cub Run

- Prescription for a backed-up drain

All marriages have their moments—some tense and some funny. I chose to include "chuckable" moments from couples representing a range of ages. A few examples of what you will experience from Marriage Moments, Part 3, includes:

- How to get a husband to realize that you mean what you are saying

- What not to do when your car breaks down on a busy highway and you know your wife will drive by shortly

- The consequences of turning your wheels out while parking on a hill

- The training of dust bunnies

The world of doctors, hospitals, and medicine does not usually make a person smile or chuckle. There are, however, things that happen in the medical arena that are funny. You just have to look for them. In Part 4 of *Chuckles: Mild to Severe*, you will discover:

- The IRS transplant

- New names for your dentist

- Things you might say after being prepped for a colonoscopy

- How to avoid the doctor if….

Part 5 observes the strange messages we get in life when people and organizations compress the English language. When messages are shortened and/or words are placed in incorrect positions, the intended meaning is lost. I call these "mad messages." For example: Mr. Brown operates a snow removal service. "Brown Snow Removal" is the ad listed on the side of his trucks. The wording suggests he removes brown snow. And we all know what brown snow is. Some additional "mad messages" in Part 5 include:

- Restrooms are incorrectly named
- The meaning of BOO-POO
- How to cement a relationship
- License plate spotting: PE4US

A variety of my stories do not fit neatly into the previous book parts and they are not connected to each other; therefore an appropriate name for Part 6 is Variety Pack. In this final part, you will enjoy:

- Visualizing the confrontation of the dog and substitute mail carrier
- The spider encounter
- A lean, mean, loving machine

As I committed my memories to paper, chuckles abounded as they did when I first lived them. If my stories cause you to recall pleasant memories from your past and chuckles erupt, then I will consider this book to be a success. My purpose in writing *Chuckles: Mild to Severe* was to share little doses of joy that come from "chuckable" moments. I'll keep my ears tuned to the chuckling of the world, and maybe some of it will be coming from my readers.

PART 1
Years with Students

TP

When the Armentrouts lived in Appomattox, Virginia, I served as the high school principal. Students were always looking for ways to play pranks and deliver some mischief. One Sunday evening, we returned home and started down our long driveway. As the house came into view, we noticed it had a different appearance. The two-story brick home had been wrapped in toilet paper. The strips went from the ground, up over the roof, and down the other side. It was covered! A few days later, I told the offenders that the next time they wanted to give us something, they should make it easier to unwrap and it should be softer.

Red Devil

One Saturday morning, I got a call from the principal of a school whose football team beat us the night before

56–0. He told me that someone had taken the statue of their mascot: a red devil. He said, "I'm convinced that some of your students did it."

Chuckling, I exclaimed, "The devil, you say?" He was not amused by my comment. Some principals just have no sense of humor. Early Monday morning, I contacted a few of my students and let it be known that the red devil was missing and it must be returned in perfect condition. After a few days, I got a note from the devil-napper indicating that "the devil made me do it" and it would be returned. Our students eventually did return the red devil, and Rustburg's principal was most appreciative.

Not Ready

While shopping at the grocery store, our neighbor approached me. She said, "You and your staff gave a good orientation to the incoming middle school students and parents last night. However, when we got home, Tommy asked me, 'What do I need a cup for?' He is so not ready for middle school."

Not Floss

As the first grade teacher moved around the room, she noticed a boy sitting at his desk. His shoe was off and a sock lay on the top of the desk. As she got closer to the child, it appeared that he was flossing his teeth. Standing beside the boy, she asked, "Where did you get that floss and why are you flossing now?"

He responded, "Mom always says I need to floss whenever I can. I'm using the elastic from my sock. Do you think it's okay for my friends to use it too?"

President

During a class discussion of the early American presidents, the teacher asked, "Who knows the third president?" From the back of the room came the comment, "I don't think anyone here has ever met him!"

Lily Pad

The class was on the floor for some creative exercises. The elementary school teacher directed them to pretend they were fish swimming in a pond. Participation was lively. However, as the teacher approached, Tommy sat motionless with his chin pointed toward the ceiling.

"Tommy, what are you doing?" she asked.

With great confidence he replied, "I'm a frog sitting on my lily pad just waiting to become a prince!"

Being Right

Teacher: "Joan, this is the seventh time I've had to correct you. What do you have to say about that?"
Joan: "Yes, it is nice being right seven times."

I'm Leaving

One of my responsibilities as the high school principal was to serve as a chaperone for the senior class trip to Washington DC. As the itinerary was being developed by the class officers, I insisted that a theatrical performance be included. On the night of the performance, the seniors entered the Kennedy Center with great excitement. The cast of *South Pacific* was doing a terrific job, when a senior setting behind me said, "If they break out into song one more time, I'm out of here!"

Homework

The teacher sat down with Bart to discuss last night's homework. "Bart, may I see your homework, and don't tell me the dog ate it again."

Bart responded, "Mrs. Smith, I offered it to the dog, but he wouldn't even sniff it."

Last Name

The teacher gave her third graders final directions for the assignment. She explained, "And, class, make sure you put your last name in the lower right-hand corner of the paper." The students completed their assignments and turned in their work. As the teacher quickly reviewed the papers, one caught her attention. In the lower right-hand corner was printed: Your Last Name

Have Class

A handmade sign posted on the classroom door read: Teacher's Hairy Class. I think the intended message was: Teacher's Have Class.

Writing

My college English teacher commented, "Mr. Armentrout, it sure is a pain for me to read your writing!"

"Yes, Dr. Jones, and it sure was a pain for me to write it for you too," was my reply.

After Graduation

Substitute teacher to ninth grader: "Johnny, what are you going to be when you graduate?"

Johnny, in all seriousness: "Probably gray and toothless!"

Minus 100

After the first math test of the school year, the teacher realized her students needed a lot of work. One student raised his hand and asked, "How did I get a -50 on this test?"

The teacher answered, "You obviously did not work hard enough!"

The student said, "So, you mean if I work harder next time, I'll get a -100?"

North Carolina

The substitute asked the students to write a few paragraphs about their homes. When finished, they selected a classmate to check the work for grammar and punctuation. Rich, who had recently moved from North Carolina, asked Jan to check his work. Jan looked over Rich's paper and said, "You need to capitalize the words North Carolina."

Rich replied, "Oh, we just don't do that in North Carolina!"

Alphabet

Father: "Son, how was school today?"

Son: "Okay. We're learning the alphabet. My teacher wants us to write twenty-six letters. I think I'll write the first one to my grandpa."

Bull Run

Teacher to class: "What happened at Bull Run?"
Student: "Was that the running of the bulls?"

Top of the Class

Charles accompanied his parents to the mid-year parent teacher conference. Charles's teacher reported that he was not exactly at the top of his class.

Charles, hearing the report, said, "That's good because I'm afraid of heights!"

Sweet Math

Teacher, "Alice, if you had five pieces of candy in one hand and eight pieces in the other hand, what would you have?"

With a smile on her face, Alice said, "Sweet delight."

Spanking

Tommy was sitting in the principal's office, waiting to hear the bad news. The principal addressed Tommy. "This is the fifth time this month you have been in my office. What do you have to say for yourself?"

Tommy thought a moment and said, "I don't want to worry you, Mr. Armentrout, but Dad said that one more time in the principal's office meant someone would be getting a spanking. Maybe I could put in a good word for you."

Pudding

As the teacher monitored her students in the cafeteria, she noticed Robbie holding his cup of pudding up to his eyes.

"Robbie, what are you doing?" she asked.

Continuing to stare at the pudding, he said, "Mrs. Jones, in class you said, 'The proof is in the pudding.' I haven't found it yet."

Pi

A substitute teacher was helping a group of seventh graders understand the geometry symbol pi.

The substitute asked the question, "Now, what does pi equal?"

A chubby girl in the front row responded, "Well, it does not equal weight loss!"

Specialist

Teacher: "Billy, what do you want to be when you grow up?"
Billy: "Well, since Mom always says I'm special, guess I'll become a specialist."

Cattle

Jean had just finished a career unit with her sixth graders. As a culminating assignment, each student was to decide upon a career path that may be in their future and write a brief paragraph explaining their choice. As Jean silently read each returned paper, the list of jobs sounded familiar. However, one paper got her attention: "I'll work the stock market, hedge some funds, and run the bulls."

Dirt Machine

As an introductory activity, the teacher said to her fourth graders, "It's important that we get to know each other. I would like you to take turns and come to the front of the room. Tell us your name and something you enjoy doing." The students remained silent and thoughtful. A boy suddenly jumped out of his seat and stomped to the front of the room.

"I'm Kevin. I'm a lean, mean, dirt machine! I know how to make playing in the dirt an art form. Any questions?"

Rearin

Two teenagers were adamantly complaining about family rules. The boy said, "When I'm an adult, I'm raising my kids with no rules!"

The girl replied, "Rearin is the correct word."

The boy asked indignantly, "Did you say something about my rear end?"

Pantry Raid

Each year, elementary schools hold a spelling bee. The child who wins gets a prize and will probably do well as a student for many years. What happens to the child who comes in last in the spelling bee? In one case, the answer may be seen in a college freshman's e-mail: "Dude, tonight we're going to have a pantry raid on Gifford Dorm. Spread the word!"

Chemistry

In high school, my friends would ask me what I was going to do when I graduated. I told them I would be a chemical engineer. It sounded like an impressive job title, and I would probably make a lot of money. Then I took chemistry.

Pollinator

I had a friend in college who had a strong Y chromosome and thought of himself as God's gift to women. He once compared himself to a honeybee: "I fly from flower to flower gathering all the sweetness. In fact, some call me the Pollinator."

Graduation Day

At our son's high school graduation, I was embarrassed at the behavior of the seniors as they threw beach balls throughout the ceremony. Later in the afternoon, I drove to the Shenandoah Valley for the graduation of our godson. This ceremony was quite dignified. When the principal declared them to be graduates, only one senior threw his mortar board into the air. The principal shot him a stern look. Interestingly, that boy, eventually, became his son-in-law.

Mom Says the Same

One day I conducted a teacher observation in an eighth grade science classroom. The teacher was explaining a weather concept. The teacher explained the concept three times. From the back of the room came the question, "Did you say something, Mr. Boyd?"

Mr. Boyd responded, "Jerry, if you did not get it during the first three times, just forget it!"

Jerry said, "You know, that's exactly what my mom tells me!"

Will She?

After a long school year, graduation day finally arrived. As the high school principal, I conducted the outdoor ceremony, which included the awarding of diplomas. My daughter was in line waiting for her name to be called.

I wondered how she would react when her turn came to accept her diploma from me. Would she laugh and hug me? Would she call me Daddy and give me a kiss on the cheek? Then the time arrived, and I called her name. She walked confidently across the farm wagon (stage), calmly took the diploma, shook my hand, and quickly left the stage. Then out of the corner of my eye, I saw a lot of activity among seniors near the stage. They were passing money back and forth. Apparently, there had been many wagers on whether Jan would kiss her father. Furthermore, I noticed that she was receiving some money. I had never before looked upon a high school graduation as an event worthy of wagers.

Running Back

As the Appomattox County High School principal, I served as a chaperone on eleven senior class trips. It was a twenty-four hour per day responsibility. Student safety was my first concern. My safety was not an issue. That leads to a story that will explain why I will never forget what the football position of running back means. On one of the trips, we were enjoying some down time in a hotel parking lot. The senior boys talked me into playing offensive lineman for the touch football game. The game started and my team had the ball. The quarterback handed the ball to his running back, and he ran right. The offensive linemen also ran right. Suddenly, I found myself on the concrete and it felt like someone had just ran across my back. The game stopped. Seniors gathered around their principal, who lay face down. The boy carrying the ball hurried back to my side. He said, "Mr. Armentrout, are you all right?"

I slowly turned over, carefully planning my words to the senior. "Gus, I have just one favor to ask you. When you got to college next year, don't ask the college president to play touch football with you."

He chuckled and then asked, in all seriousness, "Sir, will this keep me from getting my diploma next week?"

I noticed he looked pale. I looked at him and said, "Only if it happens again." A week later, he marched across the stage and got his high school diploma.

The Faculty Follies

In the late seventies, the faculty of Broadway High School held a show for the student body and community. It was called the Faculty Follies, and it ran for three nights. This was an opportunity for the teachers and principals to show off their talents and at the same time have some fun. As an assistant principal, I dressed up in Bermuda shorts and a yellow rain coat, and rode a tricycle across the stage. Then, intentionally, I ran into the piano at center stage, paused, and toppled over, completing the well-known routine from *Laugh-in*. The audience howled as students hurried to pick me up and carry me off the stage while my legs were still wrapped around the tricycle.

This next act is fondly remembered by everyone present. As the curtain rose, one spotlight focused on a commode sitting on top of a platform in the center of the stage. Steps led up to the throne. Toilet paper was on the handle. At stage right, another spotlight was on the head football coach, who was wearing a toga and a crown. In his right hand he gripped a scepter. He just stood there looking in the direction of center stage. The audience went wild with laughter. He slowly turned to the audience and took one step toward center stage. The audience got louder. Then with determination, he moved toward center stage and slowly up the steps. With hysteria filling the auditorium, the king turned toward his audience and finally sat on the throne. He reached for the toilet paper. He wiped his ... nose.

PART 2
Family Laugh Appetizers

Give Me a Minute, Grandpa.

On a long road trip with our eight-year-old grandson, we played the alphabet game. You start by looking for something outside the car that starts with the letter "A" and move through the alphabet. Each passenger takes his turn respectively. As we traveled down the road, our grandson did well, but the letter "U" became a challenge for him.

Finally he shouted out, "Underwear!" I reminded him that it had to be something you see outside the window.

I heard a commotion in the back seat. Looking in the rearview window, I saw him taking off his belt. Then he said, "Grandpa, give me a few minutes and then roll down the window!"

Chalk and Walk

When I was young, Dad enjoyed telling me about his old girlfriends. He said he especially liked the "healthy" girls. When I inquired what he meant by "healthy," he answered, "Those with meat on their bones. There was one girl I had to chalk and walk. I would hug her and make a chalk mark on her side. Then move a little and hug and mark her again until I was sure I got all the way around."

Ball Vine

One afternoon we took our year-old grandson to our tomato patch. When he saw the tomatoes, he reached down and started picking them. With one in each hand, he looked up and said, "Ball, ball!"

His father replied, "Now Owen is going to think this is where balls come from: the ball vine."

Parakeet

The boy's birthday was approaching and he was eager to find out what his parents were going to give him.

"Sis," he said, "I think I know what Mom and Dad are getting me this year."

"What's that?" she asked.

"A parakeet," he answered.

"How do you know?" his sister inquired.

"Mom said she was going to Birds, Bath, and Beyond to get it," was his answer.

Wet Dog

For Christmas our friends gave us an aromatic machine. Rich inserted the disc, and a pungent aroma quickly filled the room. "What is that smell?" I demanded.

Rich said, "It's wet dog. Doesn't it do something for you?"

"Yes, I've got the urge to throw Rover in the tub and lather him up," was my answer.

Cold Ears

Rich and I got up early one Saturday morning and drove to Carlyle, Pennsylvania, for a car show and flea market. We arrived midmorning and started walking the endless rows of vendors. The morning was getting colder and colder. It did not take us long to realize our lightweight clothing was insufficient. We had neither gloves nor hats, but, for a while, our interest in looking for "fleas" overshadowed the cold breeze hitting us in the face. I covered my ears with my hands as we walked around. I said to Rich, "My ears are so cold, I think they'll drop off. I've got to find something to put on my ears to keep them warm!" He suggested looking for a vendor with clothing. Luckily, we spotted a woman with possibilities on her sales table. I quickly started rummaging through the stack and found a pair of gloves. I held them up, wondering if I should put them on my hands or if somehow I could wear them on my ears. Then I spotted a pair of Bermuda shorts. I held them up for Rich to see.

Rich started laughing and said, "I know what you're thinking. Don't do it!"

I said to Rich, "I don't care how stupid this will be. I've got to cover my ears."

Rich replied, "You'll look like an idiot, but an idiot who has warm ears. By the way, you'll have to walk the rest of this flea market by yourself. And if you see the police, run." Just then, a frigid blast of air hit me in the face. It was put on or shut up time. I put the Bermuda shorts on my head, positioning the waist around my ears. Then I took off my pants belt, strung it through the loops of the shorts, and tightened it. The legs of the shorts drooped over like rabbit ears, giving additional protection. I knew it was not pretty but didn't care. As I started down another row, I looked back to see Rich, who was rolling on the ground with laughter. As I walked around the flea market with my newest creation on my head, it was obvious that people wanted to keep their distance.

I guess I learned something about myself that day: I'll go to great lengths—or shorts—to keep my ears warm.

Get Up

One day, little Ellen and her dad were having some play time. He went across the floor on his hands and knees pretending to be a horse. Ellen was riding on his back. After a few times around the room, she asked, "Does this hurts your knees?"

He looked up at her and said, "Sure does!"

"Then get up, stupid!" she replied.

Take a Number

As I approached the dating age, I asked Dad how he met Mom. He explained, "Your mom came from a large family of girls. There were so many sisters that a busload of guys showed up at their house in the Gravels every Saturday night. Once there, you had to take a number to see who you got. I got your Mom."

Eye On the Ball

I was playing T-ball with our twenty-month-old grandson. He had been swinging the bat at the ball and hitting a lot of air and occasionally the T-ball stand. "Owen," I said, "keep your eye on the ball." He paused a minute and then moved closer to the T-ball stand. Slowly, he tilted his head forward and put his eye on the ball.

Self-Sanitized

The toilets in Germany can be surprising. I sat on the commode seat and noticed it was wet and sticky. When nature's call was finished, I pushed the button and the seat started revolving. Instantly, I reached up hoping that maybe a seat belt was available. Not finding one, I got my "cheeks" off the seat and stood in amazement as this thing kept moving around in a circle. I thought I'd lost my mind.

Park in Munich

While visiting Germany, our guide said, "There is a park here in Munich where people take their dogs naked." Before I could ask if the people or their dogs were naked, she continued, "It helps to be a little short-sighted in that park." She later commented that the annual radish shaving festival occurs in the same park. I could not help saying, "Those people in Munich sure know how to have a good time."

Five-Year Period

On our tour bus, a lady sitting across the aisle from me was working a crossword puzzle. She leaned my way and asked, "What is a five-letter word for a five-year period?"

I responded with, "I'm not sure but would guess that women would answer, 'Agony.'"

Pickups

Cousin Sonny was invited to attend the point-to-point races on a beautiful Sunday afternoon. Before the first race, he was included in a group to walk the entire race course and pick up stones, trash, and objects that the horses might step on, causing them to throw the riders. Two of the jockeys, both from Ireland, walked along and told stories from the racing circuit. As the group progressed, some were bending over and picking up undesirables. Then there was a couple ladies trying to pick up the desirables: the jockeys.

Flaming Rooster

One Sunday, we drove into the country with our family and friends, looking for a delicious brunch. Finding a nice restaurant, we sat down and reviewed the menu. I noticed an unusual listing: flaming rooster. My mind immediately formed the image of a rooster with outstretched wings, with feathers ablaze. At that instant, the waitress asked me, "Sir, what do you want to order?"

I told her, "I'll take the flaming rooster and a fire extinguisher on the side."

Out and Play

As a young family, our first home was in Harrisonburg, Virginia. When our daughter became a toddler, we would often play in the front yard, which was near postage stamp size. Frequently neighborhood children would come down the sidewalk and join us in the fun. One afternoon, my wife and I heard a gentle knock on the door. Opening the door revealed a small boy with arm extended, ready to knock again. The boy said, "Is he ... ugh. Can that man come out and play?"

Lawnmower

When we lived in a row house in Harrisonburg, Virginia tenants had yards about the size of a postage stamp. Whenever I needed to cut the grass, I used a pair of handheld grass clippers. The job would take me about ten minutes. One day, I heard a lawn mower start up. It was loud and sounded like it was outside our door. I went outside and saw our neighbor sitting on his new riding mower, cutting his grass. His lawn mower was about the width of his lawn. He got on the mower, turned it on, and turned it off. He was done.

Turn It Up

The mother had received an electric keyboard for her birthday and was thoroughly enjoying playing music from her past. When her son came in the door from school, he said, "Mom, I heard you playing halfway down the street!"

With a smile, she replied, "Okay, I'll turn the volume up a bit!"

Sleep

Brothers and sisters habitually razz each other, especially during the teen years.

After an evening of watching television, the sister announces, "It's time for me to go to bed. I need my beauty sleep."

Brother, unable to let that line go, said, "Sis, sleep is not a miracle worker!"

Syndrome

Our teenage daughter enjoyed having girlfriends visit on a regular basis. They seemed to be able to talk nonstop.

Several would be talking at the same time. Could anyone be listening? I could not resist asking my wife, "Is there such a thing as restless tongue syndrome for girls?"

I Could Give Up

Everyone was feeling the effects of the recession and looking for ways to cut back. My wife and I decided to develop a list of some money-saving strategies. My list included things I could give up:

- Eating, but the waist would waste away
- Deodorant, but fainting in the office is not good
- Golf, but then again, I'm not a quitter

New Solution

One morning, I stood at the bathroom sink, going through my routine. Things were going as usual until I started taking my pills. With frustration, I watched my laxative pills spill into the bathroom sink. Then suddenly I realized: this may be a new solution for backed up drains. I may never need to call the plumber again.

Fingernails

We hosted two young girls for a week during the summer. Jackie and Lindsay (ages nine and ten) loved to dress up. Their fake fingernails added to their "grown-up" appearance. I finally asked them, "Can I try on those fingernails?"

Their response was, "Silly! They don't make fake fingernails for seniors." Boy that hurts.

Dressed Up

Through the years, I've dressed up to impersonate Santa Claus, Chris Columbus, and Thomas Jefferson. Later I advanced to the Easter Bunny and Buzzy Bee. I never really minded people laughing at me. Maybe my DNA is twisted. I actually didn't look too bad in the Donald Duck orange tights.

Eljan

Our son had just told us that they were expecting a bundle of joy. My wife and I immediately started thinking of names for a boy or girl. Combining the first names of both grandmothers would create Janelle. My wife said, "You could turn the name around and have Eljan. The nickname could then be Watch."

Winter Underwear

My parents-in-law enjoyed playing with words. When Johnny Frank went about his tasks, one could hear the old favorite songs being sung with a few new words. One

Christmas, Edith hosted the United Methodist Women for a Bible study. Because he possessed a pleasant voice, Johnny was asked to sing for the group. He started with "Winter Wonderland," using the words everyone knew. Then some changes were made as he sang, "What a beautiful sight, walking in my winter underwear." All the old ladies giggled with delight.

Will Shortly

Several families waited patiently in the hallway to tour an elegant Victorian home. A woman approached the group and said, "Your tour guide will shortly be with you. Thanks for being so patient."

A little boy looked up at his dad and asked, "Do we call the guide by his first name or last?" The Dad looked puzzled by his son's question. "You know, Will Shortly!"

Faucets

We had taken family members to Cass, West Virginia, to ride the train and enjoy the area. As we waited at the train station, David was sitting on a bench, patting a dog. My wife sat down beside him and asked, "David, what kind of a dog is that?"

The four-year-old replied, "Grandma Ellen, it's a female."

"How do you know?" Grandma Ellen asked.

"Cause she has faucets," was his answer.

One Leg

We reminded Grandpa Frank that his five-year-old grandson was very outspoken and to keep that in mind while they were at the grocery store. The shopping trip was uneventful until Kevin and Grandpa Frank reached the checkout counter. Kevin started staring at the man in front of them.

"Grandpa," Kevin announced in a loud voice, "that man has only one leg!"

"Kevin, be quiet," Grandpa insisted.

The man turned around, smiled at Kevin, and said to Grandpa, "It's okay. You should have seen the reaction of my son when he realized our neighbor had two legs."

The Exhibit

One Labor Day, the Armentrout family went to the National Zoo in Washington DC, so our young grandson could see the animals. There were hordes of people at the zoo on that beautiful day. As we toured, it appeared that many of the exhibits were without animals. I just assumed they were at the beach and dreading their return home for the work week. As I approached a small indoor exhibit at the monkey house, I noticed there were no inhabitants. However, there was one cement block in the center of the living area and a spotlight was shining on it. I overheard a father comment to his young son as they stood looking through the glass, "Son, I guess this is a cement block exhibit."

The son asked, "What does it do?"

Local Color

When my wife and I travel, we enjoy eating in small towns. By eating at the mom-and-pop restaurants, we get a feel for the local color. To me "local color" refers to the habits and customs of the local residents. One day, we were driving on a scenic route in Virginia and made our noontime stop for lunch in a small town. We went into the town's only eating establishment, which was filled with talking patrons. The noise level approached a middle school cafeteria at high noon. A man walked over and took our order. As soon as he turned his head and started to walk away, he let out a burp that bounced off the walls. The conversation level in the room immediately lowered to a near whisper. I said to my wife, "Now, that is control! I should have tried that technique as a middle school principal."

Duct Tape

E-mail message from a friend: "Today, I kept the kids tied up while I finished dusting. That reminds me, I'm out of duct tape!"

Had she used the duct tape for tying up the kids or for dusting? I wondered.

Bad Cold

My wife had been suffering with a cold for several days. She sat across from me with her nose running and eyes watering. I asked if there was anything I could do for her. "My nose needs a diaper and my eyes need a windshield wiper. Do they make them as a combo?" she asked.

Exciting

We had a birthday party for our four-year-old grandson. As the evening progressed, it was harder and harder for Davey to contain himself. At one point, he stood on a chair, and with a big smile, proclaimed, "I'm so exciting!"

A Question for the Manager

One hot summer day, Cousin Charles and his family had just sat down at a restaurant in Alabama when six topless young men came through the front door asking to be served. The manager walked through the nearly unoccupied room and addressed the men. After a brief conversation, the manager left the room and quickly returned with a box. From the box, he pulled out shirts, which the men donned, and they were quickly seated. The manager then walked over to Charles's table and said, "I hope you were not disturbed by that incident. It doesn't happen often."

Charles stood up and whispered in the manager's ear, "Is this a good time to tell you I'm not wearing any underwear?"

Leg of Snow

Two young brothers excitedly ran into the house to tell their mother the news of the big snow. The older brother said, "We probably got a foot of snow!"

The younger brother, displaying evidence of snow up to his waist, replied, "A foot! I think we've got a whole leg."

The Gun

When we lived in Broadway, Virginia, my wife and I had precious little time for ourselves. We had two small children, and I was an assistant principal at the high school. We were desperate for a baby-sitter. Our prayers were answered one evening when a teenage girl knocked on our door. She introduced herself and offered her services to watch our children. Over the next few years, Susan was our steady baby-sitter. One evening, we decided to go out to eat and leave the kids with Susan. We were almost at the restaurant when I remembered my wallet was at home on the dresser. We quickly drove home, and upon entering the front door, could hear loud voices coming from upstairs. We hurried up the steps and stopped at the shut door. Susan's voice rang out, "Put down that gun! Please put down that gun?"

I opened the door to see a stream of water being enthusiastically shot across the room and landing on Susan. Our son was in the bathtub, aiming the water gun at her, and had successfully pinned her to the back wall. Susan was dripping wet and wearing a smile. She looked at me and said, "He's got a good aim for a four-year-old. The next time we do this, I'll bring an umbrella."

I said, "The next time you do this, you may need your bathing suit and a mop."

The Plate

In the summer of 1957, my teenage cousin spent a week with our family in Keezletown, Virginia. One evening after supper, Grandma handed Cousin Judy a plate filled with scraps of food. Grandma's instructions were, "Take this plate and throw it across the fence by the creek." Judy ran out the back door, and within minutes, returned to Grandma's side.

"Where is the plate?" Grandma asked. "I threw it across the fence, just as you told me," was Judy's reply.

Moon Risings

During the hot days of summer, we country boys were attracted to the cool waters of Cub Run. We enjoyed jumping off the creek bank and cannon-balling into the water. The goal was to get the water to splash as high and far as possible. We did this for hours. This activity eventually became a contest with maximum exposure. It didn't take long for one boy to bear all, and the rest of us followed. Since our favorite swimming hole was not far from the highway, the skinny-dipping generated a lot of interest as people drove home from work. It did not matter to us. We kept on, even until the moon rose over the Massanutten Mountain. Yes, there were a lot of moon risings along that creek bank.

Granny Legs

As a child, there are certain functions you never expect to see your granny perform. As a young girl, my wife walked into the laundry room and found her granny with one foot firmly on the floor and the other resting in the sink. With razor in hand, she was carefully shaving her right leg. Granny says, "Susie, come on in. I'm shaving. Bet you didn't know I could do this. I'll know I'm getting old when I can't throw my leg up and over into the sink and get rid of this briar patch." It was a sight to behold.

Longevity

My wife's uncle enjoyed giving a standard response when people asked him his age. He would explain, "My grandfather lived to the age of ninety-five. My father lived to the age of ninety-eight. Now, I'm one hundred and one years old. So you can see, I come from a family of long livers." He would then pretend to start unbuttoning his shirt and continue, "Would you like to see mine?"

With Bells On

For months, my wife's cousin, Nathan, had been planning his trip to Virginia. We had not seen him for years and were not sure we could recognize him. We also wanted to make a good first impression, even at the airport. Prior to his flight from Washington State, our last communication stated, "We'll be there with bells to greet you." Before we left for the airport, my wife made an attractive sign with his name on it. I went to the attic and pulled a string of Christmas bells out of a box and tied them to my belt. Then, it was off to the airport. From the minute we got out of the car, heads started turning our way. Inside a large corridor, a man yelled to me, "Hello, Mr. Jingles!"

We arrived at the correct gate and waited. As people started through the gate, my wife held up the sign, and I started moving my hips. The hip movement sent the sound of ringing bells throughout the area. Most passengers simply ignored us. Some smiled, chuckled, and kept moving. Finally, a man paused, looked at the sign, and walked over to us. He stopped and said, "I'm not Nathan, but can I come home with you?"

We did eventually unite with Nathan, and he was quite pleased with the reception. The stranger did not come home with us; however, I think it gave him some ideas for welcoming friends.

I'll Take It

When my mother-in-law lived with us in Appomattox, she decided to have a yard sale to dispose of her household goods. We made all the plans, and on a Saturday, the bargain shoppers appeared. About midday, a close friend approached me, carrying a jewelry box.

Rich said, "How much is this jewelry box?"

I answered, "It's $10."
Rich said, "I'll give you $12."
I said, "I'll take $8."
Rich countered, "I'll give you $15."
I responded, "I'll take $7."
Rich said, "My last offer is $18."
I told him, "I'll take $5."

This unusual bantering caused a crowd to form around us. One man, standing next to Rich, pushed forward and said loudly, "I'll take it for $5.00 since he obviously does not want it!"

Long Commute

Since it takes me three and a half hours to mow and trim our yard, I always set out a small cooler with a bottle of cold water to quench my thirst. One day, after finishing the yard, I grabbed the cooler and headed for the house. Our neighbor called out, "Do you always carry your lunch with you to mow the yard?"

"Yes," I replied. "It's such a long commute."

Glori

Cousin Charles's daughter was asked to be the flower girl in a wedding. The daughter seemed reluctant to participate until she realized that another girl would be joining her with that assignment. During the rehearsal, the two girls became good friends. On the way home, I asked the name of her new friend, and she said, "Glori."

Charles said, "Yes, and years from now she will be called Old Glori."

Dog Needs Help

We had taken our dog to the family reunion. The young children really enjoyed him. They tried to get on his back, pulled his tail, and tried to get him to play soccer. He finally hobbled over to me, sat down, and looked up. I could read his mind: "Got a Prozac handy?"

Photographic Equipment

We had just finished our meal at the dinner theater when a man stepped to the front of the stage with announcements. He went through his spiel, which included, "And no pornographic equipment is allowed." He instantly realized his blunder. He stopped, smiled, and said, "And also no photographic equipment is allowed." The disappointed audience chuckled.

Baby On Board

Two new mothers were talking. One said, "You know that bumper sticker that reads, 'Baby On Board'? I used to think it was alerting drivers to be extra careful to avoid accidents. I was wrong. It means, get out of my way! The baby is screaming and I'm coming through."

Pizza to Go

While eating at a local restaurant, I noticed a funeral procession moving slowly down the road. I was surprised to see that the third car had a pizza sign on the top. I can only assume that the deceased had made an order "to go."

Overkill

My wife and I had gone to the funeral home to pay respects to a friend. We arrived on time but we were the only people there. We waited and waited and no one came. I found the funeral director and ask him if there had been some confusion about the viewing date and time. He explained that the family had requested morning, afternoon and evening sessions. I turned to my wife and quietly asked, "Isn't that overkill?"

Mules

"And when I was fifteen, I used a mule to plow out the potatoes," I told some family members.

My cousin asked, "Where did you get the mule?"

"A rental agency called Mules by Hurts," was my reply. *Heehaw!*

Like Dad

We went shopping for larger clothes for our two-year-old son. My wife, being an excellent shopper, knew how to find quality, functionality, and a bargain price. She asked Kevin, "Do you like these jeans?"

He glanced at them and said, "No man hole. I want a man hole!" Guess what he got.

Too Good At This

The harried mom was glad to see Friday come to an end. She crossed her arms and looked down at her active six-year-old.

"Sammy, I'm going to have to punish you again. This will be the tenth time this week. What do you have to say for yourself?"

Sammy said, "Mom, I think you're getting really good at this! You can quit any time."

Hearing Test

Mother to third grader: "Did you have the tests today?"
Son: "Yep!"
Mother: "What were the results?"
Son: "I had an eye test and a hearing test. The teacher said I got a 20/20. So that means 20 on each. Guess I failed."

Idiots

While visiting the local book store, our nine-year-old nephew searched the database for books of interest. One book got his attention. The company name had the word *Idiots* therein. Josh asked, "Why is that name used?" I told him it was a unique name used to sell books. His response, "It didn't work for me!"

Easter Eggs

At our outdoor picnic, I explained to my cousin how to keep a yard healthy and beautiful. I compared the attractiveness of our yard with the neglected condition of the neighbor's yard.

"How bad is the neighbor's yard?" asked my cousin as he started gawking across the fence.

"Last year they hid Easter eggs. The grass was so tall it took them three days to find the kids!" I explained.

Beltway

The family was sitting around the dinner table after a big Thanksgiving meal. The discussion topics included children, politics, and food. At the mention of food, Tom said, "I have eaten so much, I forgot my beltway."

"What is your beltway?" asked Beth.

"Well, in the morning when I put on my pants, my belt will have a way to go to get to its final destination," answered Tom.

Evaporated Milk

One day, Grandma asked me to walk to the store and get some milk and eggs.

"Grandma, what kind of milk do you want?" I asked.

"Jackie, bring me two cans of evaporated milk," was her reply.

I thought for a few minutes and then inquired, "Why do you want two empty cans? The milk is already evaporated!"

Short Cut

I grew up in Keezletown, Virginia, and I always got my hair cut by the woman at the end of the lane. I disliked long hair, and she could be trusted to cut it short. She had cut my grandfather's hair and my father's hair. As years passed, she also cut my son's hair and eventually my grandson's hair. Some years ago, the county of Rockingham named the graveled road to her house Miss Elton Lane. It seemed appropriate since it resulted in a short cut.

Names

At a party, the hostess looked at her friend and said, "Sylvia, I want you to meet the Armentrouts." Sylvia immediately started laughing. I guess she thought the name was funny. The hostess quickly continued, "And this is my friend, Sylvia Higgenbottom." It was hard not to chuckle.

Dryer

My wife and I had to find a way to do the laundry and get our grandson to sleep at the same time. Solution:

- Put him in the car carrier
- Place carrier and occupant on top of clothes dryer
- Place clothes in dryer
- Turn on dryer
- Dryer vibrates
- Baby sleeps

Spanking

The child was being spanked.

Mother: "Susie, you've got to learn!"

Susie: "But do I have to be spanked each time I learn something?"

Reception

At a wedding reception, I overheard two small children talking about the event. The girl said, "The bride was so beautiful. I'm going to be a bride someday."

The small boy, wearing a suit and tie, looked at the girl and replied, "Yes, and someday I'll be your broom!"

Dawn

As a family, we had just spent an enjoyable day at the park. The two young brothers were talking nonstop as we walked back home.

Older brother: "Let's see if Dad will take us again tomorrow. We'll play all day."

Younger brother: "Okay. I heard the park's open don 'til dust."

The Market

I heard two small children talking in the grocery store.

Girl: "Mom said we lost money in the … something. I don't remember what!"

Boy: "I think you mean the stork market."

Drainy Day

Our daughter sat looking out the window as the rain persisted. Gloom was written over her face as I approached. "What's wrong, dear?" I asked.

"Nothing, Dad. It's just a drainy day. You know, dreary and rainy-drainy."

Short Ranger

One summer, we toured Virginia Civil War sites with our Western cousins. At one national park, we were assembled, waiting for the tour to begin, when over the public address system came the announcement, "Ladies and gentlemen, shortly a park ranger will conduct a brief tour of the battle grounds." Our quick-witted cousin turned to me and said, "Sounds like the tour will be led by a short park ranger wearing briefs." And then, there he was. The ranger was about five feet tall. He had a big smile on his face. Was it because he heard the comments or because he was wearing briefs? We'll never know.

Pirate

Family members have always known that I enjoy dressing up in costumes to play a role or make people laugh. Once I was asked if I ever dreamed of being a pirate. I honestly answered, "No. Besides getting seasick, I'm not too big on the earring thing."

Apples

One fall day, we took Jan to an apple orchard. Our purpose was to gather enough apples to make a few pies. The owner said we could have any apples lying on the ground. A close look revealed that many of the apples were rotting. We therefore explained to our young daughter what to look for. After a few minutes, our daughter came up to us with her bucket filled with apples. Glancing at her apples, I noticed each one had a bite taken out of it.

I asked, "Darling, didn't we tell you to get only the good ones?"

She answered, "Yes, Daddy, that's why I tasted them!"

The Volcano

The father had just finished building a small paper-mache volcano for his son. As the boy watched, vinegar was added to baking soda and the two-year-old witnessed his first volcanic eruption. The eruption was caught on a large cookie sheet instead of the carpet. The boy was thrilled, and for weeks thereafter, he brought up the subject on a regular basis. As Christmas approached, the parents took their son to see Santa at the local mall. While sitting on Santa's lap, the boy was asked the famous question by the jolly old man: "What do you want for Christmas?"

The boy quickly replied, "A big volcano!"

Santa looked in the direction of the parents, and after receiving an affirmative nod, said, "Yes, I will see that you get it."

The boy climbed down from Santa's lap and stood at Santa's black boots. He did not move. He just kept looking up at Santa. His mother called out, "Owen, come over here. What are you waiting for?"

Owen answered, "I'm waiting for my volcano!"

PART 3
Marriage Moments

It Works For Husbands

As a trainer of substitute teachers, one day I was explaining the broken record technique to a group. I explained that in using the technique, you repeat the same words several times to the misbehaving child. This is in an effort to get their attention and let it be known that you mean what you are saying. I casually mentioned that the technique can also be effective with teenagers at home. From the back of the room came the comment, "Yes, and it works well with husbands too!"

Sampler

Shortly before Valentine's Day, my wife stood in the aisle of the retail store holding a box on her left shoulder. The box was three feet long and two feet wide. In bold letters were the words: Whitman's Sampler. I told her, "Honey, if you want a box that is not a sampler, I'll have to go home and get the truck."

Missing Truck

When our front doorbell rang, my wife went to open the door. She was greeted by a man offering roofing services. The contractor stated, "Lady, maybe you have seen my truck around the neighborhood."

Without a smile my wife said, "No, have you lost it?"

Hydrants

A married couple moved from Northern Virginia to a town in Alabama. Always being civic-minded, they decided to attend a meeting of the town council. At the meeting, the mayor gave a very detailed maintenance report on the town's fire hydrants. His report lasted about twenty minutes. He ended by saying, "So, council members, I'm glad to report that all four hydrants are in good working order."

Passing By

Dad's truck died on him as he drove home from work. He was able to pull over to the shoulder. He wasn't concerned because he knew Mom would be coming down the road in a few minutes. She could stop and take him home. When he saw her car at a distance, he started waving his arms. The closer she got, the more animated he became with waving and shouting. He could see her looking straight ahead. Mom's car approached him and then passed by. She had not even looked his way. Dad walked back out of the road and exclaimed, "She wouldn't have seen me if I had been standing here bear naked."

The Hill

Mom took a taxi home. She came through the door in a flurry.

"Mom, you seem upset," I stated.

"You see, I was parking my car facing down the hill. I can never remember which way to turn the wheels, so I turned them out. Suddenly the car started moving so I opened the door. I hardly had time to get out of the car before it rolled down the hill and hit the tree," she explained.

Niagara Falls

We decided to celebrate our fortieth wedding anniversary by driving to Niagara Falls. As we were leaving the driveway, friends drove up to wish us a safe and enjoyable trip. Ron said to me, "I know you went there on your honeymoon. Guess this time you will actually see the Falls."

"Maybe," was my reply.

Caverns

My wife and I were college sweethearts. One weekend we decided to tour a local caverns. We joined the last tour of the day. Before entering the caverns, the guide explained to the group all the necessary procedures and safety precautions. I noticed he was not carrying a flashlight and asked him about it. He indicated that the lighting system had recently been upgraded and we had no reason to be concerned. The tour commenced with the guide stopping periodically to point out prominent structures. At one point he said, "We are now at the lowest point of the caverns …" Then the lights went out. It was pitch dark.

My sweetheart grabbed me and said, "Oh, knight in shining armor, I sure hope you have something that shines!"

Dust Bunnies

House cleaning is low on our must-do list, but adding humor helps. One morning we worked for two hours cleaning the downstairs. I heard my wife say, "I hear the dust bunnies calling me from the top of the dresser. Tell them we'll get to them after lunch."

We left for lunch and met a friend while there. After chatting, I told the friend, "We must go. The dust bunnies are calling."

The friend responded, "I've got a dust bunny insight for you. The secret is in the training. I've trained mine to call the maid service."

Manners

In rearing our children, my wife and I always stressed the importance of showing respect and displaying good manners. At the end of a family meal, we taught them to say, "May I please be excused? And thank you for supper." Those manners traveled into the twenty-first century and reappeared at the dinner table one Sunday evening with our son's family. Our grandson had eaten well and was ready to get down from his chair. His father looked across the table and said to his son, "Say, 'May I please be excused?'"

My wife quickly followed with, "And thank you for supper!" Our two-year-old grandson responded with, "You're welcome."

Yard Sales

We enjoy Saturday morning yard sales in the town of Warrenton, and recently we experienced one like no other. These people had everything extremely organized, with customer satisfaction the goal. There were circulating fans inside the garage, for-sale items neatly displayed with easy-to-read prices, many people available to answer your questions, and refreshments. The girl operating the food stand regularly called out, "Get your free lemonade here: only twenty-five cents!" When we first approached the yard sale, yellow tape stretched across large sections, restricting parking. Immediately, a teenager, wearing a reflective vest, walked in our direction and asked us to park in a freshly mowed parking spot. I had the distinct feeling that the next time these people have a yard sale, they will offer valet parking.

Nose

One afternoon, while hugging my wife, I inadvertently put my nose in her eye (sure does spoil a romantic moment). I apologized. She said, "That's okay. I don't usually see a person's nose unless he has a honker. But this time, I did get a good look at yours!"

Spitting

Each Tuesday, my wife does the ironing. She says that it is important to have an iron that has the right features for the task. A lot of extra bells and whistles gives the iron its own personality, and sometimes that personality is obnoxious. For example, one day the iron started spitting water out its "nose" onto the shirt she was ironing. She said, "I've had to put up with this iron too long. It spits whenever it wants to. It will shut off anytime it wants to. It also has too much heft." We decided to give the iron its last rites and sent it to its eternal home: wherever obnoxious irons go for eternity.

We went out the door and drove to our local department store, which had several models on display. A sales representative approached us and asked, "How can I be of assistance?"

I said, "We want just a simple, lightweight iron, one that stays on until my wife is done, but most important, an iron that does not spit."

He smiled and said, "You may want this model. It is guaranteed not to spit. However, it does chew from time to time." He then bent over with laughter, and we chuckled.

Bladder

Husband to wife: "My bladder seems to shrink in the evening. I'm always going. Does that happen to you?"

Wife: "Yes, it comes with getting older. Just don't climb a ladder after 5:00 p.m."

Butts Only

As we got out of our car at the antique shop, a man was sitting on a five-gallon bucket next to the entrance. Approaching the door, we noticed the sign next to the bucket: Butts Only. It certainly looked like he was complying.

Expire

As we were going through the mail, we noticed a copy of our favorite magazine. My wife said, "Look at the magazine and find out when we expire."

I responded, "I hope not anytime soon. I don't think we're ready!"

Teeth

The men gathered each Saturday morning at McDonald's for their coffee. Today the discussion topic moved into the arena of desire. Each man contributed his example of what made his wife desirable. Then a gray-haired man shared, "There's nothing sexier than a woman who sleeps with her teeth under the pillow!"

Raisins and Prunes

As we ate lunch, my wife and I overheard a discussion between two elderly gentlemen. Each was talking loudly.

Man #1: "When you were a boy, what kind of raising did you get?"

Man #2: "I never get raisins, only prunes."

Hair in Sunlight

One day as we ate lunch, my wife looked at me and said, "Your hair looks so good in the sunlight." Taking her words as a compliment, I was ready to thank her when she added, "I really like the sunlight."

Rattling Water

Grandma was playing on the floor with her six-month-old grandson. Grandpa was observing the action and said, "Grandma, he is drooling so bad, he's got to be thirsty. Get him some water."

"Don't you know he only drinks rattling water?" responded Grandma.

"What's rattling water?" asked Grandpa.

"Let me tell you the secret to making it. Pour tap water into a tippy cup. Add ice. Shake. Give it to the baby. Baby shakes it. Rattling water!" explained Grandma.

Snail

Harry was lying on the couch when his wife, Shirley, stomped into the living room. "When are you going to mow the yard?" she demanded. "It's beginning to look like a jungle."

"Honey, you know that once I get started, I'm like the energizer bunny," he proclaimed.

"You're more like an energizer snail, if you ask me."

Nightses

With a handful of freshly pulled flowers, the child hurried from the garden into the house.

"Mom, I just picked you some nightses!" shouted the boy.

"Thank you, darling. These daises are quite nice," Mom replied.

Eyelashes

TV commercials show models extending their eyelashes to astonishing lengths. My wife commented, "If they get any longer, they'll be able to part their hair."

Manager

As we entered the grocery store, I noticed individual pictures of the management team posted on the window. Each person had a caption listing their area of responsibility. Then I saw the caption "Non-Perishable Manager." I told my wife, "That guy is going to be around a long time!"

Give Blood

After giving blood one morning, I was surprised to still be feeling strong. So I went home cleaned, vacuumed, and dusted. When I was almost finished, my wife came up to me and commented, "I guess you should give blood more often."

PART 4
Medical Briefs

Mayo Clinic

Coworkers were having lunch together and lamenting.

Darlene tells June, "And my hips, knees, and feet have been bothering me for a month!"

June replies, "And I have a constant head and back ache. Should we schedule a spa day or check ourselves into the Mayo Clinic?"

Root Canal

The main event of my day had been the root canal surgery in the dentist's office. Later in the evening, our son called and inquired about my condition. He asked, "And what is the extent of your pain?"

My response was, "Well, son, it extends from my jaw all the way to my bank account."

Transplant

It seems that a top-level politician has failed to pay income taxes again. A news media reported that he recently entered a local hospital. I'm guessing he's in for an IRS transplant.

Emptied

One of the more common reasons to go to the dentist is to get a tooth filled. So why don't we hear anyone say they went to the dentist to get a tooth emptied?

Names for a Dentist

I've often wondered how the word *dentist* evolved. Considering the type of work a dentist performs, I believe there are more appropriate vocational titles. Examples might include:
> Gum caretaker
> Electric drill operator
> Root and stump remover
> Pain specialist
> Masked man

Menopause

This word is so misleading. It suggests that it has something to do with men. Shouldn't it be called womenopause?

Wrong Doctor

You know you have chosen the wrong doctor when the information sheet asks for the *patent's* name.

Colonoscopy

As I get very tired and weak, silly things pop out of my mouth. My recent colonoscopy prep and procedure set the stage for a few comments:

The hospital registrar inquired of my condition. I told her, "I'm in the final stage of the process, the end game."

To the nurse about to roll me into the procedure room, I said, "I'm ready to get this behind me!"

To another nurse, who oddly asked about my frequent physical activities, "I run a lot!"

Hurt All Over

My father-in-law was short in stature but long on wit. One day, he was not feeling well and declared, "I feel sick all over. Sure glad I'm not any bigger!"

Bladder

Without fail, every time I visit the library and spend time in the stacks, a certain feeling comes over me. It starts with claustrophobia and ends with bladder shrinkage. Where is the men's room?

Bill of Health

Doctor: "All the test results and the physical exam indicate that you are in good shape. I'm giving you a good bill of health."

Patient: "Don't tell me that, doc. I've had friends who got a good bill of health and died the next week!"

PART 5
Mad Messages

Relaxed Fit

The tags attached to clothing can pose a problem in your decision-making process. The tag on the jeans said "Relaxed Fit." I guess that means you wear that size when you're bloated or pushing husky?

Restroom

Women's restroom. Men's restroom. Where did those words come from? They certainly do not reflect function. Wouldn't it be more appropriate to call them sit and go rooms?

Ghosts

A vanity Virginia license plate reads "BOO POO." I had never realized that ghosts have "POO TOO."

Don't Touch

Sign on a store push cart: "DO NOT Touch. Will Kill."
Now that is a clear message.

Blender

Message on a kitchen blender: "16-speed blender."
    Any more speeds and I'll mount it on my bicycle.

Gripes

Sign on customer service island in a department store:
"Want only good gripes."

Resistant

Sign on expensive shot glass: "Break resistant."
    I first read the sign as beak resistant. My mistake.

Framed

Sign in picture department: "Buy One—Get Framed."
That might be a little risky.

Colanders

Sign indicated a collection of colored collapsible colanders. I bet you can't say that correctly five times.

Epoxie

Sign on a business in a strip mall: "Weddings by Epoxie." Now that's how to cement a relationship!

Timer

In a department store, I found this listed: "Apron timer." Does anyone know why an apron would need a timer?

Pans

The close-out sign in the department store chain listed many items with great reductions. One listing included burnt pans.

I hope they mean bunt pans.

Bumper Sticker

The license plate read "PE4US." I couldn't decide if it was a personalized tag for a physical education teacher or a urologist.

Sponsored By

I did not realize that some toilets had sponsorships. In the men's room at the local theater was a sign reading "Toilet sponsored by Harry SeaMore."

Van

I've been a license plate collector for years. So while I am driving around, I am checking out license plates. It is not unusual to find creativity expressed on vanity plates. Recently a large, attractive, white van passed me, and the letters on the plate were VANNA WH

Happy

Bumper sticker on back of a car: "Be Happy Damn It."

Welcome

Hand painted sign at the marina: "Welcome A Broad."

Snow Removal

Sign on a truck: "Brown Snow Removal."

Does this mean Mr. Brown's snow removal or brown snow removal? The punctuation makes the difference, as does the snow content.

PART 6
Variety Pack

Spider

At the campsite, the boys finished unpacking their gear. I announced, "Scouts, we have a modern convenience this weekend: an outhouse. I'll check to see if it is usable." I walked to the weather-beaten structure and slowly opened the wobbly door. Instantly, I was eyeball-to-eyeball with the largest spider I'd ever seen. The extensive web covered the doorway, and the spider was claiming its territory. Suddenly out of my mouth came, "Sorry, I didn't know it was occupied. I'll wait my turn!" I backed out and called to the scouts, "I need a volunteer!"

Dirty Rat

In the summer of 2009, the news reported that Minnie Mouse had been groped by a man who was vacationing at

Disney World. It shows that groping has fallen to a new low. I guess the man could officially be called a dirty rat.

Spitting Splinters

Two dogs were sitting on a front porch.

Dog 1: "How's your day going?"

Dog 2: "Not good."

Dog 1: "What do you mean?"

Dog 2: "You know how much I enjoy chasing the mailman. Well, today there was a substitute carrier. He came through the gate, and I started the shock and awe treatment. I pinned him back against the fence and went for his leg. When my teeth entered the leg, I knew something was wrong. The man had a wooden leg. He quickly took it off and started beating me over the head with it. What a headache, and I'm still spitting splinters.

Officer Negative

An article in the local newspaper was titled "Cat Shot By Officer Negative for Rabies." Could this mean that Officer Negative shot the cat?

Segway

The man brought his Segway back to the store. He approached the salesman and, in a frustrated tone, said, "I don't mean to be so dumb, but show me where the gas goes."

Totem Pole

What do you call a young totem pole? A totem stick.

A.D.D.

When asked on Facebook, "You A.D.D.?" I felt compelled to inform them, "Yes, and also S.U.B.T.R.A.C.T."

Poke

My grandmother told me that in her youth, the word *poke* referred to a bag. On Facebook, I keep getting poked. Does that mean I'm being bagged?

COW

Sometimes, living in a rural area presents its own unique set of problems. It was fall in the Shenandoah Valley, and I was attending a civic meeting. The men began talking about the approach of hunting season. One man said to me, "Last year, I had three cows mistaken for deer. They were shot by hunters who did not know the difference between a cow and a deer. Maybe they were just drinking too much. Anyway, this year, I've decided to teach the hunters a lesson and protect my animals."

"What are you going to do?" I asked.

"Drive by my farm the week before hunting season begins and you will see," was his reply.

So, two weeks before hunting season, I drove down the road leading to his farm. In the distance I could see animals grazing in the fields next to the major highway. Something looked different about these animals. Then, I could see the results of the farmer's work. He had painted large, white letters "COW" on the sides of each animal. No cows were sacrificed that year.

Lean, Mean

Teenage boys always have a big ego, and I was no exception. "Lean, mean, loving machine," my ego talking when I was a senior in high school.

Wimps

In January, President Obama called the people in the Washington DC area "winter weather wimps." If you are the principal of the private school where his girls attend, the president's message would ring loud and clear: Whenever there is a question about closing school, who do you call? It's not Ghostbusters.

Bailouts

The irresponsible behavior of some top CEOs has led to massive bank and insurance company bailouts by the federal government. Rather than bailouts, I'd like to see some jail-ins.

Quitting Time

I entered the jewelry store around noon one Monday. As I handed the jeweler my wristwatch, I said, "My watch says it is five o'clock. I think something needs to be done." He looked at my watch and then his.

He thought a moment, smiled, and said, "You're the man I've been looking for all morning. Let's trade watches. You see, I get off at five. See ya!"

Chipper

Two wood chippers were talking one day. One said to the other, "And this is my son. He is a chipper off the old block."

Jeep

I drive a 1992 Jeep with over one hundred and ninety-nine thousand miles on it, most of which were there when it joined the family. Each November, it has to go to the Jeep hospital to make sure it is healthy and safe for another year. As I sat in the waiting room one year, it crossed my mind that this may be the year to put the Jeep to sleep or retire it to another worthy family. Suddenly, the door opened and the doctor came into the room with a puzzled expression on his face. I asked, "How's the health of my Jeep?"

He replied, "Looks like you put some miles on it this year."

"Yes. About seven hundred. I guess I was a bit excessive. I've learned to like putting the rubber to the road."

Mailbox

I never cease to be amazed by people who share their personal behavior and misdeeds with the public. Recently, I overheard a salesperson talking with a customer friend. The salesperson was explaining, in a rather loud voice, that she had an encounter with a policeman on the previous day. She said, "I told the officer that my car had done only a little damage to the mailbox. I just flattened the back end of it. I'm sure it can be straightened out. The post is only in two pieces. Anyway, people should stop planting their mailboxes in the middle of the road."

EPILOGUE

The experience of writing *Chuckles: Mild to Severe* has been both satisfying and challenging. Somehow, placing these stories in print made me reconnect with the people, times, and events. Their importance to me has increased. I will continue to keep my chuckles radar in working condition, scanning daily events for information worthy of a chuckle or two. I hope you will find little doses of joy each day from "chuckable" moments.